PEEBLES
-2 FEB 2012

3 0 MAR 2012

SCOTTISH BORDERS COUNCIL
LIBRARY AND INFORMATION SERVICES
ST MARY'S MILL
SELKIRK
TD7 5EW

Tel: Selkirk (01750) 20842
This book is due for return on or before the last date stamped
above to any library within the Scottish Borders.

Scottish Borders
COUNCIL

Titles in Full Flight 6

Hard Drive Boy	Jonny Zucker
Robot Safe Crackers	Jonny Zucker
Blood Wheels	Stan Cullimore
Surf Attack	Alison Hawes
The Dream Catcher	Jane A.C. West
Framed!	Jillian Powell
House of Fear	Tony Norman
Go-Kart Crazy	Roger Hurn
Spirit Tribe	Melanie Joyce
Lunar Rover	David Orme

Badger Publishing Limited
15 Wedgwood Gate, Pin Green Industrial Estate,
Stevenage, Hertfordshire SG1 4SU
Telephone: 01438 356907. Fax: 01438 747015.
www.badger-publishing.co.uk
enquiries@badger-publishing.co.uk

Go-Kart Crazy   ISBN 978-1-84691-668-7

Text © Roger Hurn 2009
Complete work © Badger Publishing Limited 2009

All rights reserved. No part of this publication may be reproduced, stored in any form or by any means mechanical, electronic, recording or otherwise without the prior permission of the publisher.

The right of Roger Hurn to be identified as author of this Work has been asserted by him in accordance with the Copyright, Designs and Patents Act 1988.

Series Editor: Johnny Zucker
Publisher: David Jamieson.
Editor: Danny Pearson
Design: Fi Grant
Cover illustration: Pete Smith

GO-KART CRAZY

Contents

Chapter 1
The Die-Hard Trophy page 4

Chapter 2
What a Let Down! page 9

Chapter 3
Kart Mart Smart page 13

Chapter 4
Break Down! page 16

Chapter 5
Race Against Time page 20

Chapter 6
Surprise! Surprise! page 24

Chapter 7
Blast Off! page 27

Chapter 8
Fight to The Finish page 29

Badger Publishing

Chapter 1
The Die-Hard Trophy

Blaine Davis gave his go-kart engine one last tweak.

It sounded good, but Blaine was nervous.

The final of the Die-Hard Trophy was just a few days away and he badly wanted to win it.

His best buddy, Rick grinned at him.

"Relax mate. You're the best go-karter ever. Trust me - that cup is as good as yours."

Blaine wasn't so sure.

He was a great driver all right, but his kart was well past its sell-by date.

His Dad had bought it second hand and
Blaine had worked on it for months.

Now it was in tip top condition,
but it was still old.

The big question was would it last forty
flat out laps of the Silverstreak track?

Silverstreak was famous for its tight
turns, scary s-bends and super fast
straights.

And Blaine wasn't the only one to have
doubts about the kart.

"Give it up now, Davis. You've got no
chance of winning in that clapped out
old heap."

The sneering tones of Jordan Black, Blaine's arch rival, cut into Blaine's thoughts.

It was as if Jordan had read his mind.

Rick answered for him. "Push off, Jordan. Blaine's the real deal. He doesn't need a fancy kart to win."

"Just as well," replied Jordan. "Cos that wreck's no match for the brand new turbo-charged Lightning Bolt my Dad bought me. You'll be eating my exhaust fumes on Saturday, Davis. And that's a promise."

Blaine shrugged. He wasn't going to let a spoilt rich kid like Jordan get to him.

"Whatever. I'll see you at the starting grid."

Jordan grinned. "Maybe you will and maybe you won't," he said nastily.

Then he walked away.

Chapter 2
What a Let Down!

Blaine put Jordan's weird threat out of his mind.

But on the night before the race, Blaine's dog Rex started barking like crazy out in the back yard.

Blaine leapt out of bed and ran outside.

Rex was pulling hard on his chain.

Blaine was just in time to see a shadowy figure climbing back over the wall.

Blaine set Rex free and the dog bounded across the yard.
The figure dropped out of sight just before Rex could grab him.

"Good boy, Rex," said Blaine as he scratched the dog's ears.

"You scared that guy off before he could do any harm."

But then Blaine saw the garage door was open. He kept his kart in there. Blaine's heart lurched.

What had the mystery intruder been up to?

Blaine's worst fears came true.

When he walked into the garage he saw that all four tyres on his kart had been slashed.

"Oh no," he gasped. "I can't afford to buy new tyres.
What am I going to do?
I'm out of the race for sure now!"

Chapter 3
Kart Mart Smart

Blaine's Dad came running out of the house to see what all the fuss was about.

What he saw made him mad.
"Who do you think did this, son?"
he asked.

"It must have been Jordan," said Blaine. "He knows he can't beat me fair and square. So this is his way of stopping me taking part in the big race on Saturday. And he's succeeded."

But all was not lost. Blaine's Dad had a plan.

"I'm not mega rich like Jordan's dad," he said. "But I've got a few quid saved up for a rainy day. It'll be enough to get you four new tyres."

Blaine could hardly believe his ears.

"That's wicked, Dad.
I'll pay you back somehow, I promise."

Mr Davis smiled. "Forget it, son.
It'll be worth it just to see the look on Jordan's face when you turn up ready and able to blast him off the track."

Blaine nodded. "Yeah, I'll be the last person he'll expect to see."

Then Blaine groaned and put his head in his hands.

"But the race is tomorrow afternoon. We'll never be able to get the tyres in time!"

Chapter 4
Break Down!

Luckily, Blaine's Dad didn't give up easily.

He went on the internet and found a place called Kart Mart.

It sold everything to do with go-karts. But the shop was over seventy miles away.

"Set your alarm clock for 5am, Blaine," said Mr Davis. "We're going to have to leave early if we're going to get there and back in time for the start of the race."

At the crack of dawn, they loaded Blaine's kart into the back of Mr Davis' old van and set off to Kart Mart.

When they finally got there it was like an Aladdin's cave for go-karts.

It had everything - including the tyres Blaine needed.

The men at the shop helped Blaine fit them and soon Blaine and his Dad were back on the road again.

But Blaine was worried.

Time was passing quickly, but the van was going slower and slower.

"Can't you go any faster, Dad?" he asked.

"Course I can," said Mr Davis. "You're not the only top driver in our family. Watch this!"

Mr Davis put the pedal to the metal, but then disaster struck.

The engine screeched.

Thick black smoke poured out from underneath the bonnet and the old van juddered to a halt.

It had broken down!

Chapter 5
Race Against Time

Blaine was in despair.

He had no chance of making it to the Silverstreak track in time for the race now.

Mr Davis put his arm round Blaine's shoulders.

"Sorry son. I did my best, but I guess it just wasn't meant to be.
It looks like that Jordan is going to win after all."

Blaine sighed. "Never mind, Dad.
I'll get him next year - maybe."

Before Mr Davis could reply, a truck pulled up behind the van.

Two men with the Kart Mart logo on their overalls jumped out of the cab and walked over.

"What's the problem?" asked one of them.

"It's this old van of mine," replied Mr Davis. "It's had it."

"That's not the problem," groaned Blaine.

"The problem is that I need to get to Silverstreak pronto.
I'm in the Die-Hard Trophy race."

The men stared at Blaine.

"Hey, you're the kid whose tyres we fixed, aren't you?"

"You got it," said Blaine. "But it's all for nothing now."

"No way," said the man. "Rob and me are going to Silverstreak right now."

"Kart Mart is the sponsor of the main event."

"And we're the pit stop crew.
So if you and your kart want to hitch a ride to the track with us you're more than welcome."

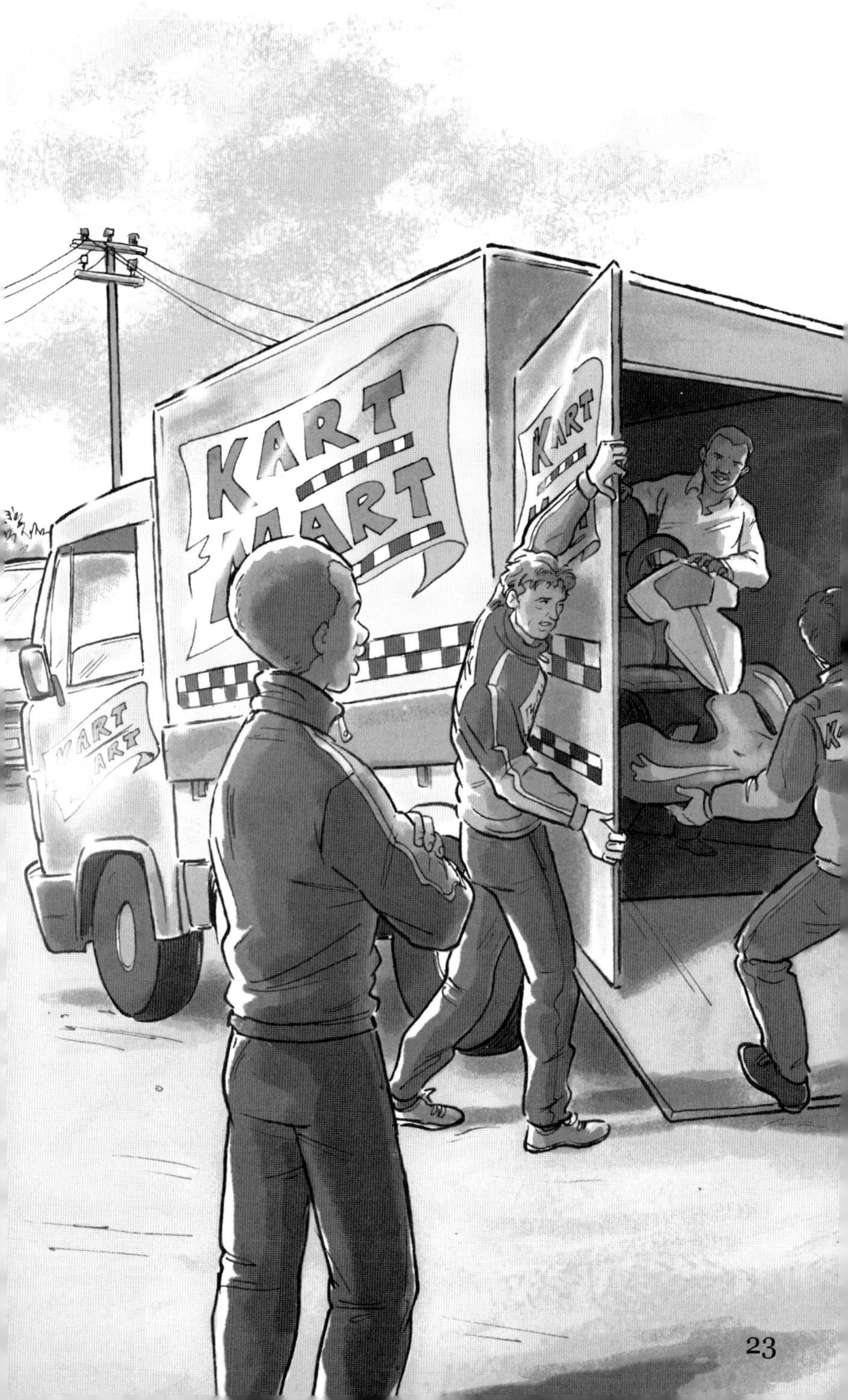
KART MART
KART
KART MART

Chapter 6
Surprise! Surprise!

Rick's heart sank when he saw Jordan strolling over to him.

"No sign of your mate, Blaine then?"

Rick looked glum and shrugged.
He had no idea where Blaine was.

"He'll be here soon," he muttered.

"No, he won't. He's bottled it," sneered Jordan.

"I guess he's just too ashamed to turn up to race in that old wreck of his. He knows I'll beat him."

Jordan felt someone tap him on the shoulder.

He turned and came face-to-face with Blaine.

His mouth fell open in surprise.

"What are you doing here?
There's no way …"

"Yeah, there's no way I should have been able to get new tyres for my kart. But I have and no thanks to you, Jordan."

"You're little plan to keep me out of the race has failed. So now you're going to have to face me on the track…"

"And may the best karter win!"

Chapter 7
Blast Off!

Twenty mean machines blasted off from the grid and raced round the track.

Blaine was right behind Jordan as they hurtled into the first hairpin bend.

Jordan took it too fast. His rear wheel lifted and he slid out wide.

Blaine saw his chance and slipped past on the inside.

He was in the lead. He stamped his foot to the floor and roared away.

Jordan raced after him.
Blaine was the better driver, but Jordan's kart had more power and speed.

Blaine knew it was only a matter of time before Jordan swept past him.

Chapter 8
Fight to The Finish

For thirty-nine laps, Blaine used all his driving skills to keep Jordan at bay.

His hands ached from gripping the wheel.

He was tired, but he knew he only had to hold on for one more lap.

The final turn was just ahead.

Then Jordan made his move.

He pulled alongside Blaine.

They were neck and neck.
Then Jordan tried to force Blaine off
the track.
But he mistimed it.

Jordan's front wheel clipped the
corner. His kart spun out of control and
crashed into a wall of tyres.

Jordan's race was over.

Blaine sped on over the finish line.
He'd won.
The Die-Hard Trophy was his!

But as Blaine went up to get the cup, he heard a strange clunking sound.

He looked back at the track and saw Jordan pushing his turbo-charged Lightning Bolt kart over the line. He had finished last.

Blaine smiled. Jordan scowled.

But both karters had got exactly what they deserved.